Reality .. A True Copy

A Three-Act Play

To watch the play, please scan the following QR Code:
Reality .. A True Copy

Dr. Sultan bin Muhammad Al-Qasimi

Reality .. A True Copy

A Three-Act Play

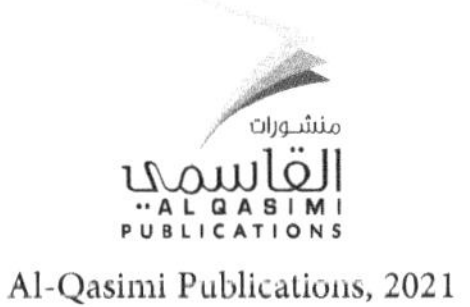

Al-Qasimi Publications, 2021

Reality .. A True Copy - A Three-Act Play

First published in 2006 in Arabic as "Alwaqie Suratun Tibqu Al-Asl"
by: Al-Qasimi Publications
Author: Dr. Sultan bin Muhammad Al-Qasimi (United Arab Emirates)
Publisher Name: Al-Qasimi Publications
Sharjah, United Arab Emirates
Edition: First
Year of publication: 2021

Translated from the Arabic by: Dr. Ahmed Ali

ISBN: 978-9948-469-56-8
Printing Permission: National Media Council, Abu Dhabi, UAE
No. MC 01-03-3836665, Date: 05-08-2021

Age Classification: E
The age group that matches the content of the books was classified according to the age classification issued by the National Council for Media
----
Al- Qasimi Publications, Al Tarfa, Sheikh Mohammed Bin Zayed Road
PO Box 64009 Sharjah, United Arab Emirates
Tel: 0097165090000, Fax: 0097165520070
Email: info@aqp.ae

CONTENTS

Foreword

The Muslim Ummah has gone through tougher periods of struggle than what is being witnessed noawadays. Let this play be a motivation to push forward and rid ourselves of negativity and despair. Let it be a wake-up call towards unity and fighting for what is right.

-The Author-

Cast of Characters

According to appearance

- Caller
- Host
- Peter, the hermit (Butrus al-Nasik)
- Two Moroccans: Ahmed and Ali
- Sheikh Muhammad
- First Man
- Second Man
- Patriarch's Assistant
- A group of men, women, youths and children.
- Patriarch Shimon
- Pope Urban II
- Priest

- Other Priest
- Church Heads and Princes
- Commanders and Princes
- Crowds of people of different ages and sexes
- Groups: 1,2,3 and 4
- A Lame Donkey
- Qadi Abu Sa'd al-Harawi
- A Crowd of people
- Judges of Damascus
- A Group of Notables
- Sulaiman
- A group of soldiers
- A Soldier
- Another Soldier
- Corpse
- Caliph al-Mustazhir Billah
- A Notable (Man)
- A Palestinian Refugee
- Abbasid Soldiers
- Hajib
- Al-Must'li Billah
- Physician

- Voices
- Afdal al-Jamali
- Imam
- A Group
- A Worshipper
- Another Worshipper
- Sultan Muhammad
- Ibn al-Khashshāb
- A group of servants, boys, girls and entourage
- The Allepine
- A Man
- Soldiers
- A Killer
- Jerusalem Youths: Ibtahim and Eissa
- Balian
- Saladin
- Patriarch Heraclius
- Saladin' Soldiers
- A Commander
- French Girl
- Group Commander
- Announcer

- Mu'azzin
- Qadi Shamsuddin
- Emperor Frederick II
- Emperor's Entourage
- Soldiers (Franks)
- Three Christian Groups
- Two Old Men
- Al-Khawarizi Muslim Group
- Three Frank Soldiers
- Two Muslim Groups

Act One

Scene I

(Curtains open)

Caller: The City of al-Quds, in 486 AH (1093 CE)

To the right of the stage, a sign hanging with the writng 'Magharibah Quarters'. To the left, a house with the door sign 'Jerusalem Patriarch'. Through a passage in the middle of the stage Bait al-Maqdis behind can be seen

Two men enter. One is Peter the hermit, a Christian mystic who is small-built, short, dark skinned, donkey-like face, barefoot and dressed in a worn-out robe. The other is Peter's host, a Jew with sidelocks dangling on both sides of the face.

On seeing the door of the residence of the Jerusalem

Patriarch, Peter heads towards it to knock on the door, but the host prevents him.

Host: Just wait … Shortly, one of the Patriarch's assistants will come. Let's just sit here and wait.

They both sit close to the door.

Peter: My apologies for the troubles I have caused you.

Host: No need for apology. But, Peter, I have received you in my house and offered you to stay with me, and you asked me about all things regarding the Christians and others. Yet, you never answered when I asked you what you intended to do here. Every time I asked, you just said you would tell me later. You visited all the churches and did your own special investigations as you call them, and now I see you are so eager to meet Shimon, the Patriarch of Jerusalem. I know he's a devout and God-fearing man. So, what do you want from him?

Peter: I want to discuss some issues with him regarding the current situation in Jerusalem. I am hoping to get a letter from him where he requests the help of the kings and princes of the West.

Host: I am a Jew myself; but deep inside I recognize the Messiah.

Peter: Personally, I follow Pope Urban II. He was originally a Jew who convertd to Christianity. He is against Pope Clement III of Rome.

Host: Shimon, the Patriarch of Jerusalem is closely related to the Roman Church. So, please do not mention to him that I had been sent by Urban II. .. I will leave you now as I need to run some errands.

Two Moroccans enter looking exhausted. Peter eavesdrop on their conversation.

Ahmed (pointing at the 'Magharibah Quarters' sign:

Ahmed: This is it, the 'Magharibah Quarters'.

Ali (following his companion Ahmed):

Ali: We have gone through a lot to get here. It was not easy finding this place. I am axhausted. I cannot walk any longer. Let's have some rest.

The two Moroccans drop their luggage close the the 'Magharibah Quarters' sign.

A dignified-looking man enters. He greets them and introduces himself.

The Man: I am Sheikh Muhammad. I take care of all

the issues related to the Moroccan visitors of Jerusalem. And you are?

Ahmed: I am Ahmed, from Morocco; and this is my travel companion from Tunisia.

Sheikh Muhammad: So, how are the affairs of the Muslims in Morocco?

Ahmed: All is well there, al-hamdu-lilah. Continued victories. Yusūf Ibn Tashfīn crossed to Andalus with 25,000 fighters. The five Taifa Kings joined him with another 25,000 men. All these troops met the King of Castille, Alfonso, and defeated his army in Zallaqa (Sagrajas).

Ali: Sheikh Muhammad, and how are the Muslims in the East?

Sheikh Muhammad: Things are not well here. We are living in political, economic and religious chaos. We have two Caliphates: one in Baghdad and another in Cairo. They are in constant conflict. Internally, it is all bad. The Caliphs are controlled by the military who instigate troubles and fight only for power and authority to get to the throne. They do not fight to defend their peoples against injustice or external threats or aggression.

Ahmed: Why don't the wise and learned amongst the Muslims interfere to reconcile the two caliphates and end their differences?

Two men enter in a rush. They are looking for someone. One of them is holding a heavy cane.

First Man: He is still here. He could not have gone farther than here.

Second man: There he is, hiding!

First Man: Yes, this is the one who had been spying on us. You were spying on us, right?

The second man raises his cane to hit Peter who runs away and hides behind Sheikh Muhammad.

Peter: Please, protect me, Sheikh.

First Man: Let him go, Sheikh Muhammad.

Sheikh Muhammad: No, he is under my protection now. Stay away from him. He sought my help and I am protecting him.

However, the cane falls on the head of Sheikh Muhammad and blood flows on his forehead.

Ali and Ahmed are shouting.

Ali: What did you do?

Ahmed: Catch him. Do not let him escape.

Ali and Ahmed: Stop! Stop!

The two attackers run away.

The Patriarch's assistant comes out.

Patriarch's Assistant: What is going on? What was that noise?

He turns to Sheikh Muhammad and looks concerned at the sight of the blood on the later's forehead.

Patriarch's Assistant: O, Sheikh Muhammad, let me help you and tend to your injury.

He rushes into the Patriarch's residence, then comes out with a bottle of medicine and tends to the Sheikh's injury. He also turns to Peter and asks:

Patriarch's Assistant: Who is this?

Peter: I am Peter the hermit. I came from the land of the Franks to pray and worship at Jerusalem.

Patriarch's Assistant: Why are you sitting here?

Peter: I came to see the Patriarch.

Patriarch's Assistant: OK, wait a minute.

Sheikh Muhammad thanks Shimon's assistant and is about to leave:

Sheikh Muhammad: Thank you for treating me. Please, remember me to Patriarch Shimon. Ket's go, brothers.

Sheikh Muhammad and the two Moroccans leave. Shimon's assistant enters the Patriarch's residence. He shortly comes out and speaks to Peter who waited outside:

Patriarch's Assistant: Please, come in to meet Patriarch Shimon.

Both Peter and the Patriarch's Assistant enter the Patriarch's residence.

The Adhan (call for Muslim prayers) is heard from Jerusalem. People of different ages and sexes hurry to the prayers. They walk across the stage from both directions. They join the road leading to Jerusalem. When the Adhan is over, the door of the Patriarchate opens and Patriarch Shimon, his assistant, and Peter come out.

Patriarch Shimon: You are a wise man, Peter. You have diverse experience in many areas and the ability to convince others by word and action.

Peter: Holy Father, I could not hold my tears back when you were describing the condition of God's people living in Jerusalem. When I remember your words, my tears flow..

Peter starts to weel. Shimon pats his shoulder. Peter turns to Shimon and inquires in a more serious tone:

Shimon: Peter, the Merciful and Compassionate Lord will not have mercy upon us because of the sins that weigh us down. Our sins have not been wiped away yet.

Peter: I have to tell you, Your Holiness, that if the Church in Rome and the kings in the West had a credible and trustworthy informant who conveys to them of the calamaties that you have been experiencing, they would have definitely tried to provide support by word and action. Therefore, write to the great Pope and the Church in Rome as well as to the princes and kings of the west. Stamp your letters with your holy seal, and I will carry out the task of delivery. I put my faith and trust in the Lord. So, I am prepared to visit them all, beg them to help and testify before them earnestly to the terrible afflictions you are suffering. I will call upon them all to provide appropriate remedies without delay.

Shimon and his assistant look happy. Then Shimon says to Peter:

Shimon: I will write the letter.

He then turns to his assistant to say: Bring me a pen, a paper and am inkpot.

Shimon's assistant goes in to bring the requested items.

Shimon *(to Peter)*: Thank you for sympathizing with us. May the Lord protect you.

Peter: I am the Lord's servant. For the sake of healing my soul, I would not hesitate to fulfil this mission.

Shimon's assistant comes out with the writing items. Shimon writes the letter, signs it and seals it with his official stamp, which he took out of his pocket.

Patriarch Shimon: There you go, Peter. Here is the letter you requested.

Peter: Thank you very much, Your Holiness.

The Patriarch and his assistant enters the Patriarchate.

Peter stands alone on the stage. He is joyous. He turns round himself screaming and waving the letter.

Peter: I got the letter, Urban. I got it and I will bring it to you myself.

He turns to face Jerusalem. He raises his index finger and says threareningly:

Peter: I will return, Jerusalem! I will return to cleanse the holy places.

-Blackout-
-Sounds of church bells and hymns-

Scene II

(Church hymns are sung)

Caller: The Council of Clermont in central France, beyond the Alps, 1095 CE

Pope Urban II is sitting at a table. He is good-looking, tall, with a nicely shaped beard and exceedingly polite demeanour. A priest enters and addresses him:

Priest: Praise the Lord for your safe return, Your Holiness! I was so worried that the Roman Emperor may afflict any harm on you on your way to southern Italy to meet Peter as he returned from Jerusalem.

Pope Urban: I was in distress until I arrived to Pari in southern Italy. There I met Peter who handed me this letter.

Priest: And where is Peter Now?

Pope Urban: He has gone to call the people to liberate the Holy City

Priest: Could I read the letter?

Pope Urban: Sure, there it is.

The priest reads the letter, then says:

Priest: It is addressed to the Pope in Rome.

Pope Urban: I am the Pope. There is no other Pope.

Priest: But the Pope in Rome is Clement III!

Pope Urban: Who? That is Guibert the merchant ...

Priest: But he has been appointed by the Roman Emperor ...

Pope Urban: Soon, I will be sitting on the Papal seat of the Church of Rome.

Peter enters. He greets Pope Urban and the priest. Another priest enters. He approaches Pope Urban for permission saying:

Other Priest: The Council is ready. The heads of the churches and the Princes are present. Please, Your Holiness.

Pope Urban, Peter and the Priest advance. They sit on the chairs overlooking the Church court. Pope Urban stands up with a cross in his hand. He addresses the Council:

Pope Urban: Heads of Churches, Princes .. Our brothern who live in Jerusalem are in terrible distress. The letter delivered to me by the Reverend, Peter, himself, who is here with us today, speaks of the same.

(Peter stands up. He greets the Council with a nod of his head).

Peter: The LORD loveth the gates of Zion more than all the dwellings of Jacob. Beloved ones, arm yourselves. Tie your swords round your waists. Go, and the Lord be with you. I say to those accused of robbery, arson, looting and plundering, murder and other similar crimes... those who by virtue of their crimes will not enter the Kingdom of God, I say to them: provide this service to please the Lord so that such pious acts may earn you forgiveness of your sins. Let the princes and commanders come forward so that I crosses may be places on their garments as an expression of their faith and a symbol of their coming pilgrimage to the Holy Land.

Pope Urban gets busy placing crosses on the garments of the princes and commanders.

To the left of the stage, Peter is busy with the crowds entering the stage from the right to volunteer for the fighting. They includes women, children and elderly people.

A group enters. Peter asks them:

Peter: What is it that you want?

Group (1): We want to join the campaign so that our friends are not alone.

Peter directs them to where all are gathering at the stage exit on the right.

Another group enters. Peter asks them:

Peter: And you, what is it you want?

Group (2): We want to join so that we are no considered infidels ...

Peter directs them to the gathering.

A third group enters. Peter asks them:

Peter: And you, what is it you want?

Group (3): We want to join because we are burdened with heavy debts.

Peter directs them to the gathering.

A fourth group enters. Peter asks them:

Peter: And you, what is it you want?

Group (4): We do not know.

Peter directs them to the gathering and follows them himself.

Peter returns to the stage. He enters from the right side, barefoot and holding a big cross. He rides a lame donkey. He is followed by multitudes of men, women and children. Some are aged. He continues to the left side of the stage weeping, wailing and pulling the hair of his beard:

Peter: To Jerusalem … Revenge … Retrieve the holy sepulcher.

His following crowds repeat after him:

The Crowds: To Jerusalem! To Jerusalem!

-Blackout-

Act Two

Scene I

(With Curtains closed)

Caller (1):

- The crowds of Peter the hermit have perished;
- The Crusaders are marching towards Constantinople;
- The Crusaders take northern Syria by surprise;
- The Caliph in Egypt sends ambassadors to the Crusaders and requests a peace treaty with them;
- The Crusaders occupy Antioch on the Orontes River;
- The Crusaders march to Jerusalem;

- Governor of Tripoli sends a delegation to negotiate peace;
- Peace between Tripoli and the Crusaders.
- Friday, 22nd Sha'ban 492 AH (15th July 1099), the Crusaders occupy Jerusalem.

The curtains open. A group of Muslims are crying and wailing. Women throw dust on their heads.

The Group: They occupied Jerusalem! Jerusalem is now in the hands of the Franks. O, Islam! O, Islam!

(Curtains down)

Caller (2): The Diwan of Caliph al-Mustazhir Billah, in Baghdad. Ramadan 492 AH (August 1099 CE), a month after the occupation of Jerusalem.

(Curtains open)

Qadi Abu Sa'd al-Harawi enters. He is the Chief Judge of Damascus. He has a thick beard. His head, uncovered, is shaved as sign of mourning.

Abu Sa'd al-Harawi: Do you accept humiliation? Are you happy being degraded?

Some of the town's notables try to calm him down. He pushes them away with a sign of contempt. He proceeds to the middle of the stage and shouts:

Abu Sa'd al-Harawi: I am Abu Sa'd al-Harawi, the Chief Judge of Damascus. I came from Damascus with these Paestinian refugees who arrived to Damascus golding the Othmani copy of the Qur'an. They are the few who survived the Jerusalem massacre. I accompanied them so that you may hear for yourselves the atrocities they had to endure a month ago. Sulaiman, come over and tell them what you saw ..

Sulaiman: It was Friday, last month, on the 22nd. It had already been forty days of siege when they eventually entered after the men who were defending the town were killed. They came raising their swords and going from one street to the other slaughtering all the men, women and children they encountered. They ransacked the homes and destroyed the mosques.

A back curtain opens to show Jerusalem. Soldiers

are killing everyone they encounter. When the roads become empty, the soldiers gather. One of them says:

A Soldier: Let's celebrate our victory.

Another Soldier: Wait! Wait! I will bring you something to celebrate with.

The soldier leaves. Peter enters riding his donkey and holding a bottle of wine from which he drinks.

Peter: Rejoice and drink this wine as you have drunk their blood here.

A corpse on the edge of the stage seems to move and a soldier pushes it with his foot. He is aided by another. The soldiers laugh. It turns out that it is a severely injured man. He sits opposie Peter. It is Sheikh Muhammad. He addresses Peter:

Sheikh Muhammad: Peter! I am Sheikh Muhammad who defended you when you were in Jerusalem. I am the one who was injured and his blood spilt to protect you. You have forgotten me that quickly?

Sheikh Muhammad points at his forehead injury he sustained defending Peter.

Peter: Oh! Sheikh Muhammad! Hahahah!

Peter takes a mouthful directly from the bottle of wine. Then spits the wine on Sheikh Muhammad's face. The soldiers gather quickly round Sheikh Muhammad and pour their bottles of wine over his head. Sheikh Muhammad cries:

Sheikh Muhammad: Astaghfurullah! Astaghfurullah! I seek God's forgiveness!

The soldiers crowd round him again and each says:

Soldiers: I will kill him.. Let me kill him. I am the one to kill him.

Peter proceeds to take a sword from one of the soldiers. He pretends to be defending Sheikh Muhammad. He says:

Peter: No, none of you will kill him.

The soldiers stop in surprise. Peter stabs Sheikh Muhammad and says:

Peter: Because I am the one who will kill him. I will kill him myself.

Sheikh Muhammad falls down. The soldiers surround his body. They carry Peter while dancing and laughing.

A man with blood all over his clothes and hands enters. His legs are soaked in blood up to his knees. He laughs loudly and says:

Man: When we finished with the killing of everyone in the house, the mosques and the streets … men, women and children … seventy thousand of them.. We then raided al-Aqsa mosque. There, we found a congregation of worshippers in prayer. We killed them all. Ha Ha Ha Ha.

The back curtain starts to close while those present are in shock. They start to sob and cry loudly.

Abu Sa'd al-Harawi comes forward and addresses them:

Abu Sa'd al-Harawi: What use are your tears when the swords are harvesting the lives of the Muslims! I travelled from Damascus to Baghdad for three weeks. We endured the dangers of the terrible journey under the scorched sun, not to get some pity. We have come to inform the Muslim authorities of the catastrophe that the Muslims are under and in order that they interfere to stop the massacres. It has never happened before that Muslims had been degraded like this!

The Abbasid Caliph al-Mustazhir Billah, 20, white complexion, short, round-faced, joyful even when extremely angry, comes forward to say:

Al-Mustazhir Billah: It saddens me what happens in Jerusalem. I sympathize with you. Therefore, I have decided that a committee of six senior members in my court be formed. It shall be called the Committee of Wisemen. Their task is to investigate these heinous targedies.

Abu Sa'd al-Harawi is furious. He turns to one of the notables and says:

Abu Sa'd al-Harawi: Where is the Sultan Berkyaruq? Take me to him in order to get an army ready to retrieve Jerusalem.

The Notable: Sultan Berkyaruq is too busy in battle fighting his own brother, Muhammad, in northern Persia.

Abu Sa'd al-Harawi: What a farce! What a farce!

A Refugee: We should go to Egypt, to the Fatimid Caliph, al-Musta'li Billah.

Al-Harawi and his group: Allahu Akbar! O, Islam! O, Islam! O, Islam!

They exit.

Al-Harawi: La Hawla wa la Quwwata illa billah. There is no power or might except with Allah!

-Blackout-

Scene II

Caller: The Diwan of the Fatimid Caliph, al-Musta'li Billah, in Cairo.

17th Safar 495 AH (10 December 1101 CE)

The Fatimid Caliph sits surrounded by some of Cairo notables. The Hajib enters.

Hajib: The Priest, representative of the Jerusalem Christians.

A priest enters holding a cross. He shakes hands with the Caliph who sits him beside him.

Priest: O, Caliph of the Believers! We have come to you to free Jerusalem from the hateful occupation carried out by the Franks against the Holy Land.

Al-Must'li Bilah: We have tried to reach an understanding with the king of the Greeks, but he informed us that he has no authority over the Franks. He also said that those who occupied Palestine were working for themselves and they wanted to establish their own state. He says he denounces their actions and is adhering firmly to his alliance with us. As you know, our endeavours to free Jerusalem were reliant on doing so from Damascus. Therefore, our army took over Tyre. However, our work had been made impossible to continue because Ridwan, Sultan of Aleppo, engaged in fighting against his brother, Daqqaq, the Sultan of Damascus. This has led to the deterioration and weakness of our position there. Yet, we promise you we will free Jerusalem.

The Caliph then feels a terrible pain in his chest. He touches his chest and screams in agony.

Priest: May I be permitted to leave?

Al-Must'li Bilah: You may.

The Caliph screams again in pain.

The Priest leaves.

(Blackout then the lights are on again)

Caller: The Caliph is seriously ill. His health is fast deteriorating.

Hajib *(shouting)*: The Physician! The Physician! Bring the Physician!

The physician enters. He examines the Caliph, then turns to the notables and says in a sad tone:

Physician: The Caliph has died.

Notables: *La hawla wa la quwwata illa billah.* There is no power or might except with Allah! *Inna lillahi wa inna ilayhi raji'oun!* We belong to Allah and to Him is our return!

The Notables remove his outer garment and turban, then move him into the house

The Hajib enters.

Hajib (*calling*): O, Afdal! O, Son of Badr al-Jamali! O, Prince of the Armies! The Caliph is dead.

A disturbance ensues with mixed voices heard indicating the arrival of an important person.

Voices: Afdal al-Jamali! Afdal al-Jamali!

Afdal al-Jamali enters carrying a 5-year old child. He places the child on the Caliph's chair. Then he dresses him in a garment and places a turban on his head.

The Notables (*together*): Afdal, what is this supposed to mean?

Afdal: This is you Caliph, Abu Ali al-Mansur, the son of the late al-Musta'li Billah. He shall be addressed by the title: al-Āmir bi-Ahkamillah.

The child plays and hides under the garment and the turban. The Notables look at him puzzled. He bursts into crying.

A Notable: How could this child rule a state of 6-million people on the verge of marching to their enemies in Palestine?

Afdal: He will through me. I will run all the state affairs.

A Notable: You? ... Why you?

Afdal: I fought in Palestine before ...

He then turns to the people and addresses them:

Afdal: O, people! Palestine is calling upon you. Rise for the liberation war! Rise to rid it of its atrocious occupiers!

The People (*shouting*): al-Jamali! al-Jamali! al-Jamali!

Afdal (*raising his sword*): To Palestine!

The People (*shouting*): al-Jamali! al-Jamali! al-Jamali!

-Blackout-

The lights come on again.

Afdal al-Jamali appears standing with some sodliers who look defeated with the injuries and torn clothes. The soldiers shout:

Soldiers: Jamali, we need your help! We have been defeated, defeated.

Afdal: O, people! Palestine is your cause. Rise to free it. To Palestine!

The People (*shouting*): al-Jamali! al-Jamali! al Jamali!

-Blackout-

The lights come on again.

Afdal al-Jamali appears standing with some sodliers who look defeated with the injuries and torn clothes. The soldiers shout:

Soldiers: Jamali, we need your help! We have been defeated, defeated.

Afdal: O, people! Our war against our enemy is before everything else! To the battle!

Afdal al-Jamali raises his sword as he exits the stage.

-Complete blackout-

Scene III

Caller: Heavy years pass as the refugees continue to be displaced. The aggression against the Muslim lands continues. Town after town falls into the hands of the aggressors.

As the lights come on, the caller shouts:

Caller: Baghdad, the year 504 AH (1111 CE).

The Mosque of Caliph al-Mustazhir Billah in his palace in Baghdad. Friday, 14th Sha'ban, 504 AH (24th February, 1111 CE)

The Imam is sitting at the top of the pulpit. Then he stands up to deliver his speech. He begins:

Imam: Praise be to Allah. May the peace and blessings of Allah be upon his Messenger.

A man wearing a turban enters. This is Qadi (Judge) ibn al-Khashshāb. He enters with a group of Aleppo locals. Their voices get higher as the guards prevent them from entering.

The Group: Let us enter the mosque … to pray. You prevent the carrying out of the prayers in the houses on Allah!

The congregation in the mosque are disturned. Their voice are rising. The soldiers hold ibn al-Khashshāb by his arms.

Imam: O, people! Quiet, please! Quiet! The person held before you is Qadi Ibn al-Khashshāb. He has come from Aleppo with some of the locals. Ibn al-Khashshāb, last Friday, you came and attacked the Sultan's mosque. You dragged the Imam down from the Pulpit and destroyed it. I had to interfere personally on your behalf to the Sultan in honour of the Scholars, Jurists and the Hashimite *Sharif* in your company. The Sultan promised you he would send the armies to rescue Aleppo. However, you come today to raid the Caliph's mosque and in the presence of the Caliph himself?!

From behind the windows of the mosque, a group of servants, boys and girls, entourage, pass. They are carrying fine clothes, luxurious jewelery, furniture and other items. Their loud ululation, clapping and singing eclipse the voice of the Imam.

A worshipper (*to another*): What is going on out there?

Other Worshipper: This is the lady Khatoun, sister of the Sultan and wife of the Caliph. She has just arrived from Isfhan.

Ibn al-Khashshāb pushes the guards to the ground. He rushes to the wooden pulpit which is decorated with carvings and qur'anic verses, to pull the Imam down. The pulpit collapses into pieces and the Imam falls. The Aleppo locals scream in the faces of Sayyidah Khatoun and her company.

The Caliph stands up and calls for the guards:

Caliph: Guards! Arrest them. Tie them up and take them to the prison.... Where is Sultan Muhammad?

Sultan Muhammad: I am here, Commander of the Faithful! Please, fo not get angry! I beg you to forgive the people for what they have done. The whole of Baghdad has no other topic to talk about but what has nefallen Palestine!

Caliph: I am not angry because of the disturbance to my wife that just happened. I am rather terribly angry because of the shouts rising in the streets of Baghdad saying 'The Roman King is more of a Muslim than the Commander of the Faithful is'.

Sultan Muhammad: The people mean the message the *Diawan* received from the Roman King some weeks ago whaere the Roman Emperor, as you already know, called for a meeting to fight the Franks and uproot the presence completely from these lands.

Ibn al-Khashshāb: O, Commander of the Faithful! The men had been butchered; the women and children taken captive. Over seventeen month, the Crusaders occupied and destroyed three of the most renowned cities in the whole of the Levant: Tripoli, Beirut and Sidon. What force is there to prevent them from invading Damascus or Cairo soon, or even Baghdad?

The Caliph (*shocked*): Baghdad?

Sultan Muhammad to Ibn al-Khashshāb:

Sultan Muhammad: Respected Qadi! Emir Mawdud of Mosul had informed us that he would personally lead a strong army to rescue Aleppo.

Ibn al-Khashshāb: May Allah bless you, Commander of the Faithful. And you, too, Sultan Muhammad.

Ibn al-Khashshāb turns to address the Aleppo locals..

Ibn al-Khashshāb (*shouting*): Good news, Aleppo! Glad Tidings, O, Damascus! Glad Tidings, O, Palestine! Victory is coming! Victory is coming!

(The Curtains close)

-Blackout-

Scene IV

Caller: City of Aleppo, 1113 CE

The curtains open.

Soldiers enter dragging Ibn al-Khashshāb who is cuffed and shackled. They untie and release him.

An Aleppine (Aleppo local) enters from the other side of the stage. He stares at Ibn al-Khashshāb.

The Allepine: Who? Qadi Ibn al-Khashshāb?

Ibn al-Khashshāb: Yes. Ridwan, the Sultan of Aleppo imprisoned me for no crime. The only thing I did was bringing him military assistance from Baghdad. As soon as we arrived to Aleppo, he ordered all Aleppo wall gates be closed.

He then ordered me and my supporters to be arrested and imprisoned in the Castle. Since then, we have not heard anything about the army led by Emir Mawdud of Mosul.

The Aleppine: The Emir and the commanders had a disagreement and Emir Mawdud returned to Iraq with his army.

Ibn al-Khashshāb: Emir Mawdud of Mosul... the land of naphtha... does not withdraw from battle.

The Aleppine: How does this naphtha work?

Ibn al-Khashshāb: When I visited the Emir in Mosul on my return from Baghdad, I urged him to save Aleppo as I found him to be a chivalrous man. There, I saw naphtha on the right of the Mosul road. At a distance, I could see how flammable it was when they were transporting it.

The Aleppine: This is true; Emir Mawdud is chivalrous. He came to Aleppo to rescue his Muslim brothers there. But he was assassinated on Friday in the mosque.

Ibn al-Khashshāb (*screaming in shock*): What? They killed him? A nation that kills its saviour, on the day of its Eid, in the house of its Lord, is worthy of nothing less than perishing by God.

He then turn to the Aleppine and says:

I will travel to Baghdad, and ask Sultan Muhammad to send a powerful army to remove the aggressors.

The Aleppine: Take it easy, my man. A military campaign was indeed launched and the army was very strong.

Ibn al-Khashshāb: Where is it now? And what did it do?

The Aleppine: As it arrived, they found the Governor of Damascus and the armies of Aleppo and Tripoli standing side by side with the armies of the occupying enemy. They all united to fight against the army sent by Sultan Muhammad.

Ibn al-Khashshāb: The Aleppo army fought against Sultan Muhammad's forces? Shame! Shame! Shame!

The Aleppine: And, King Ridwan is sick …

A man enters. He shouts:

The Man: King Ridwan is dead. King Ridwan has passed away!

Ibn al-Khashshāb (*shouting*): O, people of Aleppo! Rise and revolt! O, people of Aleppo! Rise and revolt! O, people of Aleppo! Rise and revolt!

-Blackout-

Caller: Twelve years later.

The stage is lit.

Ibn al-Khashshāb enters. He walks proudly as he says:

Ibn al-Khashshāb: We led the revolution … and installed a new governor for Aleppo. The Franks were so arrogant beyond belief. They seized Sinai with a small army, occupied the town of al-Farama (Pleusium) and reached the banks of the Nile where they swam. They could have gone farther than this if it were not for Afdal al-Jamali who could not let that humiliation continue unpunished. .. Here in Aleppo, we were victorious over the enemy, too. We crushed them in Antioch on the Orentos River. I intervened myself to realize the unity between Aleppo and Mosul which has been recently achieved. With the will of God, this will be the seed that should grow into a powerful state, which will soon repond forcefully and successfully to the Franks' arrogance. From this place, we call upon all the senior commanders to fight the invaders and free Palestine..

A man approaches Ibn al-Khashshāb and stabs him in his chest..

Ibn al-Khashshāb, in pain, falls to the ground.

Ibn al-Khashshāb: *La ilaha illa Allah, Muhammad Rasulullah.* I bear witness that there is no god, but Allah; and I bear witness that Muhammad is Allah's servant and Messenger.

Ibn al-Khashshāb falls dead. A group of people tries to assist him while another group chases the murderer.

-Blackout-

Act Three

Scene I

Sounds of catapult shots are heard

Caller: Jerusalem on 27th Rajab, 583 AH (2nd October 1187 CE)

The Curtains open.

The bombardment continues for a short while. Jerusalem appears as it did in Act One. From the side of al-Magharibah Quarters, two youngmen from Jerusalem enter in a rush.

Ibrahim: Eighty-eight years of the Franks occupation of Jerusalem. Eighty-eight years of humiliation and degredation.

Eissa: But, it will soon be over.

Ibrahim: How?

Eissa: Saladin is coming. Saladin is coming. The shots you hear are his. They are falling on the heads of the Franks.

Ibrahim: This means that after Saladin finished with Paelstine, he headed for Sidon and Tyre, then, he returned to Asklan. And when he seized Ramla and captured its Frank ruler, Balian, he set him free. But, Ballian came to Jerusalem to lead the Crusader fighters against him. I thought Saladin would not come to Jerusalem.

(Ibrahim raises his hands in prayer)

Ibrahim: O, Allah! Shower us with Your Mercy, you are the Most Merciful.

(Silence)

Ibrahim raises his arms again and prays secretly. A flash of lightning lights the stage and the sound of thunder is heard.

Caller: Jerusalem is being bomabarded by catapult shots.

The soldiers of the Franks enter led by Balian. They are looking for Muslims.

Balian (*disturbed*): Saladin has swept Jerusalem .. *Then he asks:* How many Muslims have you managed to gather?

A Soldier: Five thousands.

Balian (*pointing at Ibrahim and Eissa*): Take those two with you.

Balian looks from the stage to see Saladin arriving with a group of his men. They advance from the beginning of the theatre hall and make their way to the stage. Spotlight are directed at them. Saladin reaches the front of the stage and looks at Balian.:

Saladin: Who? Balian? Really? You lied to me after I released you. You sought permission to go to Jerusalem to bring your wife and children. You swore you would only stay one night. And there you are, leading the armies in Jerusalem?

Balian: I am the envoy of the Franks. I came to negotiate. We are prepared to pay 100,000 dinars

Saladin holds Balian by the scruf of the neck, drags him of the stage, and points to the right side while he says:

Saladin: Look at the yellow banners flying over many of the gates of the walls of Jerusalem.

Then, he points to the left side and says:

Saladin: Look at the flag my hen are raising over the hole they made in the old wall. Whenever could a captured city dictate the terms of peace?

Some of Saladin's soldiers enter. They had captured a number of senior military commanders of the Franks. The captives kneel down before Saladin.

Balian: Your Higness, the Sultan! The city is full of countless men who have not joind the fighting thinking that you would respond to the calls of peace as you did with others.

Saladin: The Christian of Jerusalem are allowed to reside in the land, and enjoy all their civil rights. You, commanders, are fully aware that they used to write to me asking that I come to free Jerusalem from the tyranny of the Franks! Well, the Franks and the Latins who are not fighters, but wish to remain in Palestine, must only stay in the understanding that they are subjects. The fighters, though, must leave Palestine. They will be escorted to safety by my soldiers to the coast. They also each will have to pay a ransom: ten dinars for the man, five for the woman and one dinar for the child. Whoever is unable to pay the ransom will be taken prisoner. And finally, you must leave within no more than forty days.

Balian: We accept.

Saladin: Take your men and leave.

The commanders of the Franks exit.

Saladin *(to his commanders)*: Commanders, please gather so that I may give you the required instructions for the running of the affairs of Jerusalem.

A Commader calls for the soldiers. A group of them gathers.

The Group Commander: Attention!

The soldiers enter the stage and Saladin walks about inspecting them.

When the inspection is over, he stands before them and says;

Saladin: You must protect each and every house against looting. No one is to be harmed in any way. You must guard the roads and city gates. You must provide security to the Christians against any acts of aggression they may be exposed to. The team leaders will need to distribute money and animals to the sick, the old and the needy among the Franks. I advise you to pay special attention to the weak and vulnerable, to honour the women and be compassionate with the children..

As soon as Saladin finishes his address, someone's voice is heard:

The patriarch: Leave me! Let me go. What do you want from me?

The Group Commander: These are Saladin's orders ... We cannot let you leave with all this money

Saladin: What is going on?

A Commander: Sultan, this is Patriarch Heraclius. He wants to leave Jerusalem. But he is carrying with him money and Jewels. I believe we should seize what he has and use it to support the Muslims.

Saladin: No, we are not men of betrayal.

Saladin proceeds towards the Patriarch, and take only ten dinars from the box. He then waves to the patriarch to go.

Saladin: You may now leave with what you have.

A Commander (*looking at the ten dinars in Saladin's hand*): Ten dinars only?

Saladin: A promise is a promise. We're men of our word.

A girl (*shouting at the soldiers in the back of the stage*): Leave me! Let me go!

Saladin: Who is the angry girl?

The Group Commander: Mawlay! This is a French girl from among the prisoners you released. She wants to talk to you.

Saladin: Let her come.

The girls approaches Saladin and addresses him angrily:

The Girl: You killed my father! You are a murderer! You also captured my two brothers. I now have no family or carer! And then, you give me freedom only to add to my problems!

Saladin smiles and turns towards the soldiers saying:

Saladin: Bring her two brothers now and release them immediately.

Then he turns to the girl to explain:

Saladin: Your father was killed in a war he himself had started. He attacked innocent people who were living in safety. As for your brothers, I release them in honour of a girl who is in need of a carer and a helper.

The Girl: Pardon my, Sultan! My anger was mainly because of the misinformation I used to hear back home about the unjust behavior of the Muslims. I am also sad for the loss of my father. Please, forgive me.

The Group Commander: Her brothers have been released ..

Saladin (*addressing the girl*): You may join your brothers.

The Girl: I thank you profusely. You are truly an honouarble Muslim Commander. I seek your forgiveness once again!

Saladin: Where will you be going now?

The Girl: Back home.

Saladin: What will you tell your people when you get there?

The Girl: I will tell the fanatics the truth about Islam and the Muslims.

The adhan (call for prayers) is heard.

The Mu'azzin (*Prayers Caller*): Allahu Akbar! Allahu Akbar!

-Blackout-

Scene II

Caller: Jerusalem in 627 AH (1229 CE). Thirty-two years after Saladin liberated it.

On the stage sits Ibrahim resting his back against the wall where the 'Magharibah Quarters' are. He is old with grey beard.

Eissa arrives looking old, too.

Eissa: Assalamu Alaykum, brother Ibrahim.

Ibrahim: Wa Alaykum Assalam, Eissa. What is the news?

Eissa: It is said that al-Kamil, the Sultan of Egypt sent his envoy, Prince Fakhruddin Yusuf to northern Syria to negotiate with the Emperor who had arrived there.

Ibrahim: A Frank?

Eissa: Yes.

Ibrahim: Eight years ago when the Franks occupied Damietta, this very Sultan, al-Kamil, relinquished the whole of Palestine in return for their withdrawal from Damietta.

Eissa: True.But al-Kamil also fought in battle against them when they rejected his offer. They were after more than just Palestine. However, al-Kamil defeated them.

Ibrahim: Yes, but he still signed a peace agreement with them in spite of his victory.

A man (*shouting from a distance*): O, people of Jerusalem! Here is Qadi Shamsuddin, the Judge of Nablus. He has been sent to you by al-Kamil, the Sultan of Egypt and the Levant, to tell you to surrender Jerusalem to the Emperor.

Ibrahim and Eissa rush to stand up.

Ibrahim (*to Eissa*): Did you hear what I just heard?

Eissa: I did.

Caller (*entering the stage, shouting*):Here is Qadi Shamsuddin, the Judge of Nablus. He has been sent to you by al-Kamil, the Sultan of Egypt and the Levant, to tell you to surrender Jerusalem to the Emperor.

Qadi Shamsuddin enters holding the keys of Jerusalem and the agreement signed by al-Kamil and the Emperor. With him enter the Emperor, his entourage and the people of Jerusalem. They all gather on the stage.

Shamsuddin: O, people of Jerusalem. The Sultan al-Kamil signed a peace agreement with the Emperor. Here are are the terms:

- The Crusaders shall receive Jerusalem, Bethlehem, Nazareth, Tibnin and Sidon;
- Jerusalem stays as is; its walls shall not to be restored. The rest of the Jerusalem villages remain in the hands of the Muslims and no authority by the Franks shall be exercised there.
- The Haram Sanctuary including the Rock area and al-Aqsa mosque shall be in the hands of the Muslims. The Franks may only be allowed as visitors. The affairs are run by the Muslims including all the Islamic rites such as the Adhan and prayers.

However, o, people of Jerusalem.

Sultan al-Kamil has given the orders that the Adhan (call for prayers) may cease for the duration of Emperor Frederick II's stay in Jerusalem in respect of his presence.

Qadi Shamsuddin hands the Keys of Jerusalem over to the Emperor. The women present start to cry, wail and scream while the men protested through shouting and raising their voices with Allahu Akbar!

A Man: *La ilaha illa Allah!* There is no god but Allah! What is all this for? Do not surrender Jerusalem. Do not stop the Adhan in Alqsa!

He then starts to make the Adhan call.

Some groups among the crowds join in shouting the Adhan.

Crowds: *Allahu Akbar … La ilaha illa Allah … Muhammad Rasulu Allah.*

Anger breaks loose. The Imams and Mu'zzins make the Adhan prayers call, altogether.

Clashes ensue. The Jerusalem people are attacked by spears and swords. They fight back with throwing stones at their attackers.

Some get arrested, others injured, and still others killed.

The group carries their dead on their shoulders and exit chanting:

Group: *Allahu Akbar ... Allahu Akbar ...*

-Blackout-

(The stage is lit).

Caller: The agreement is put into effect and Jerusalem was at the heart of the events.

Announcer: Let the Muslims leave Jerusalem. Jerusalem shall be surrendered to the Franks.

The soldiers drive out the Muslims who are sobbing and screaming.

Emperor Frederick II is crowned. He addresses his troops:

The Emperor: Praise the Lord and thank him for completing his blessings upon you. This achievement was nothing short of a miracle. It was not through courage or war, numbers or force, that we have got to where we are today. What the Lord has granted us no other power in exitence would have been able to accomplish in any fathomable manner.

At this points, three groups of Christians start to protest.

Group (1) (*Christian fanatics*): Bethlehem has not been restored by arms; the Muslims are still in charge of the Islamic rites there. In the fifth crusade, Sultan al-Kamil offered to relinquish the whole of Palestine. We demand the annexation of the territories beyond the Jorden River.

Group (2) (*The Knights Templar*): We object to the Temple being under Muslims' custody.

Group (3) (*Local Nobles*): The orders are not effective practically.

Emperor Frederick II makes his way among the protesters.

Emperor: I am leaving to attend the Mass at the Church of Resurrection.

-Blackout-

Scene III

Jerusalem in 642 AH (1244 CE)

An old man is sitting with his mate.

Caller: O, Jerusalem! What a terrible reality!

Old Man (1): O, Jerusalem! Fifteen years of occupation and humiliation. Who is out there who can liberate you?! Look at these warring nations!

Old Man (2): O, Jerusalem! Who is out there who can bring you freedom?! Look at the divergent hearts? Who will liberate you, Jerusalem?!

The voices of two groups of men walking up the theatre aisles among the audience are heard. Each group has a leader.

The Two Groups: Jihad! Jihad!

Group Leader (1): For Allah's cause.

The Two Groups: Jihad! Jihad!

Group Leader (2): For Allah's cause.

The shouts continue.

The Old Man (*turns to his mate and asks*): What are these shouts?

Other Old man (*looking at the stage*): These are shouts of the Khawarizmia Muslims. They were a thousand men and managed to liberate the towns and drove the Frans out.

Allahu Akbar! Allahu Akbar!

Old Man: O, Jerusalem! Victory has come. Victory has come.

The Franks gather as they hear the voices .They kill the two old men.

The two groups have now reached the stage and their shouts are louder.

They engage in fighting against the Franks who are

defeated after many of them are killed in the fighting. Their banner falls on the ground. A group of Franks escapes to the audience hall.

The Two Groups: Allahu Akbar! Allahu Akbar! Allahu Akbar!

People of Jerusalem: *Allahu Akbar Kabira! Wal-Hamdu Lillah Kathira! Wa Subhana Allah bukratan wa Asila!* Allah is Great! Praise be to Allah in abundance! May Allah be glorified, day and night! There is no god but Allah! He fulfilled His promise! Gave victory to His servant! Raised the status of His soldiers, and He alone defeated the confiderates. He is the First and the Last.

While the chants continue, a member in the Franks group picks their flag off the ground and raises it. As the chants end he waves the flag to his group.

One of the Franks who escaped to the audience hall shouts:

A Frank: It is our flag. It is going up ..

A Second Frank: The Franks are winning ..

A Third Frank: Let us retun to Jerusalem …

This group of the Franks head back to the stage where they are killed by the Muslims.

The Two Groups: Allahu Akbar! Allahu Akbar! Allahu Akbar!

People of Jerusalem: *Allahu Akbar Kabira! Wal-Hamdu Lillah Kathira! Wa Subhana Allah bukratan wa Asila!* Allah is Great! Praise be to Allah in abundance! May Allah be glorified, day and night! There is no god but Allah! He fulfilled His promise! Gave victory to His servant! Raised the status of His soldiers, and He alone defeated the confiderates. He is the First and the Last.

-Curtain close-

-End-

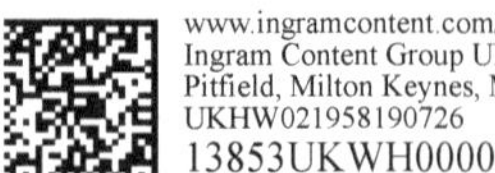

www.ingramcontent.com/pod-product-compliance
Ingram Content Group UK Ltd.
Pitfield, Milton Keynes, MK11 3LW, UK
UKHW021958190726
13853UKWH00004B/1596

9 789948 469568